The Power of Kindness and Treats!

Patricia A. Brill, PhD

Illustrated by Curt Walstead

functional
fitness
L.L.C.

Dedication

This book is dedicated to my husband, Dino Miller. He has always been the most kind and generous person I have known. I live by his example.

Hello All—

The story you are about to read is about being kind and "*paying it forward.*" My best friend Boxster taught me that it is important to be kind to one another.

He told me that real happiness comes from not what you get but what you give. When you put dogs first before yourself, good things happen. You may even get treats!

Boxster was the kindest dog I knew. He taught me the importance of doing acts of kindness. He said, "there is nothing more rewarding than the feeling of doing a good deed for someone else."

Love, Turbo

TURBO

"Turbo wake up! My birthday is in two days.
   I must go to the dog park to invite my friends. They will bring me presents and treats!"

"Slow down," sighed Turbo. "Maybe you should donate your presents to the dogs living in the shelter down the street. They have just been waiting a long time to be adopted and go to a forever home. Until then they need something to brighten up their day. Boxster taught me that it is good to *pay it forward.*"

"What does 'pay it forward' mean?" asked Porsche Bella.

Turbo replied, "*'Paying it forward'* means to reward someone's kindness toward you by being kind to someone else. Your friends coming to your party are being kind to you by bringing you presents. So why not *'pay it forward'* and donate your presents to the many dogs in the shelter that may not get to celebrate their birthday, so they won't get presents and treats?"

Turbo insisted, "Let's go to the park and invite them, but tell them that instead of bringing you presents, they can bring something for the dogs in the shelter."

All the dogs gathered around Porsche Bella.

"Hello everyone. I am having a birthday party on Saturday and I would like all of you to come."

"What do you want for a present?" shouted one dog.
Porsche Bella replied, "instead of bringing me presents and treats this year, I would like you to consider we donate to our local shelter. There are many dogs that never get treats or toys. Turbo

taught me it is better to *'pay it forward'* to those that need our help. Remember, a lot of us were in a shelter until we were adopted into our forever home and we never got presents."

"Very good Porsche Bella," assured Turbo. "Now, in addition to inviting your friends, why don't you invite some of the other dogs in the park that don't have friends."

"Why should I invite dogs I don't know?" asked Porsche Bella.
"Because you can make a difference in a dog's life and not even know it. Actions from the heart can mean the world for someone else. It is important to be selfless and do good for others" said Turbo.

Turbo pointed toward the back of the park. "Look over there. There are two dogs in the corner looking lonely and scared. They want to play but they are too shy to join in.

Take them a toy, introduce yourself, and just be kind to them. Since they do not have a friend, they may not how to respond to someone being nice."

"Hello," said Porsche Bella. "I am having a birthday party on Saturday and I would like you to attend."

"Why would you invite us?" the little dog whimpered. "No one wants to play with me because of the way I look."

"I don't see anything different about you," commented Porsche Bella. "Look at me, my body is white, but my tail is brown. Bullies would make fun of my tail. I did not want to go to the dog park, but Turbo taught me that the best thing I could do is stand up for myself and be proud of who I am."

The other dog whimpered, "No one wants to be my friend because I am in a wheelchair. My back legs don't work so well. I may be slower, but I can still do the same thing that other dogs can. It just might take me a little longer.

"We don't have any presents or treats to bring" sighed the two dogs.

"You don't have to bring anything," said Porsche Bella.

"Sometimes the best present you can give is yourself, just being there and being kind to other dogs. Kindness is a gift anyone can afford."

"How could we show kindness?" asked the little dog.
Porsche Bella explained, "you can show kindness by giving other dogs a compliment like their collar is cool or encourage

other dogs who are sad or scared with nice words, or even licks.

Small acts of kindness are likely to spread and affect others. That is, if you act kind to someone that person will be more than likely to be kind to others.

I'll see you Saturday!"

"I am so proud of you Porsche Bella," smiled Turbo. "The world is better today because you are in it. Happy Birthday!"

(Dogs at the Birthday party)

(Dogs taking stuff to the shelter)

The Power of Kindness and Treats!

© 2020 by Patricia A. Brill

Published by Functional Fitness L.L.C.

All rights reserved. No part of this book may be reproduced, stored, or transmitted by any mean (paperback)s—whether auditory, graphic, mechanical, or electronic—without written permission of the author, except for the inclusion of brief quotes in critical articles and reviews. Send inquiries to info@dogtalescollection.com.

ISBN: 978-0-9995034-2-3 (paperback)

Printed in America

Illustrated by Curt Walstead

Photo of Turbo @2016, Linda Lee Photography

Book design by DesignForBooks.com

www.ingramcontent.com/pod-product-compliance
Lightning Source LLC
Chambersburg PA
CBHW061149010526
44118CB00026B/2916